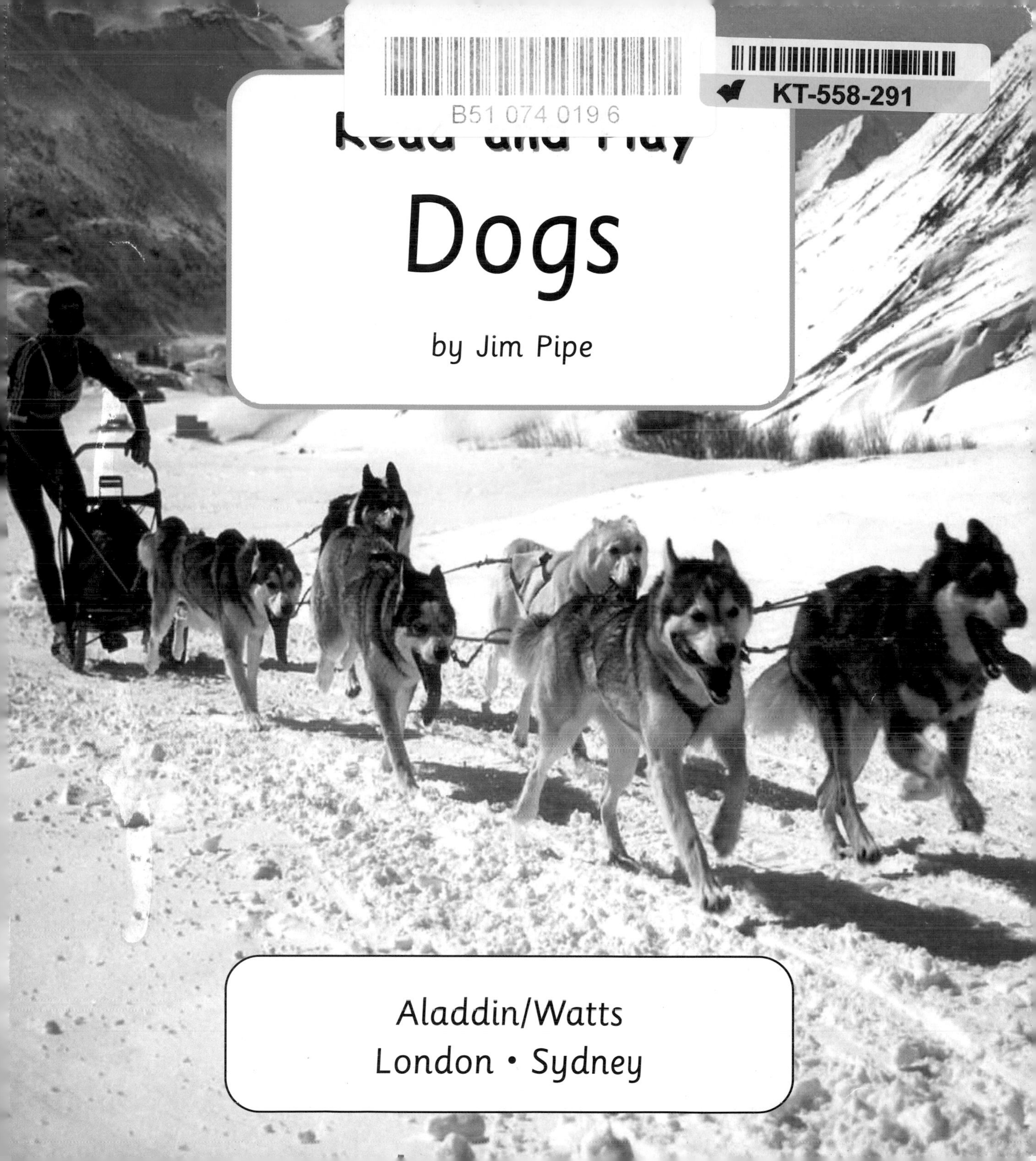

Dogs

by Jim Pipe

Aladdin/Watts
London • Sydney

dog

Some **dogs** are big.

Some **dogs** are small.

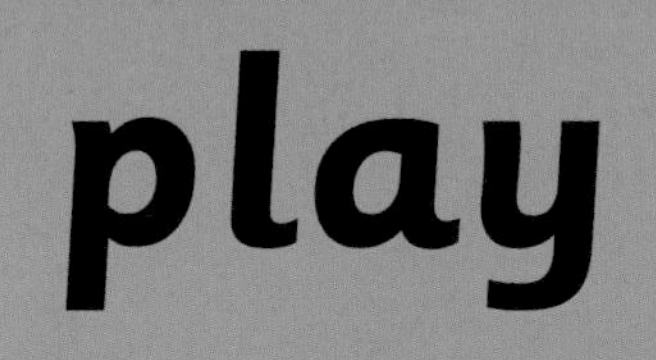

What do dogs like?

Dogs like to **play.**

puppy

A baby dog is a **puppy**.

A **puppy** likes to chew.

fur

A dog has soft **fur**.

A dog likes to roll over!

legs

A dog has four **legs**.

It likes to run and jump.

A dog has four **paws**.

It likes to dig!

tail

A dog has a **tail**.

A dog wags its **tail.**

nose

A dog has a wet **nose**.

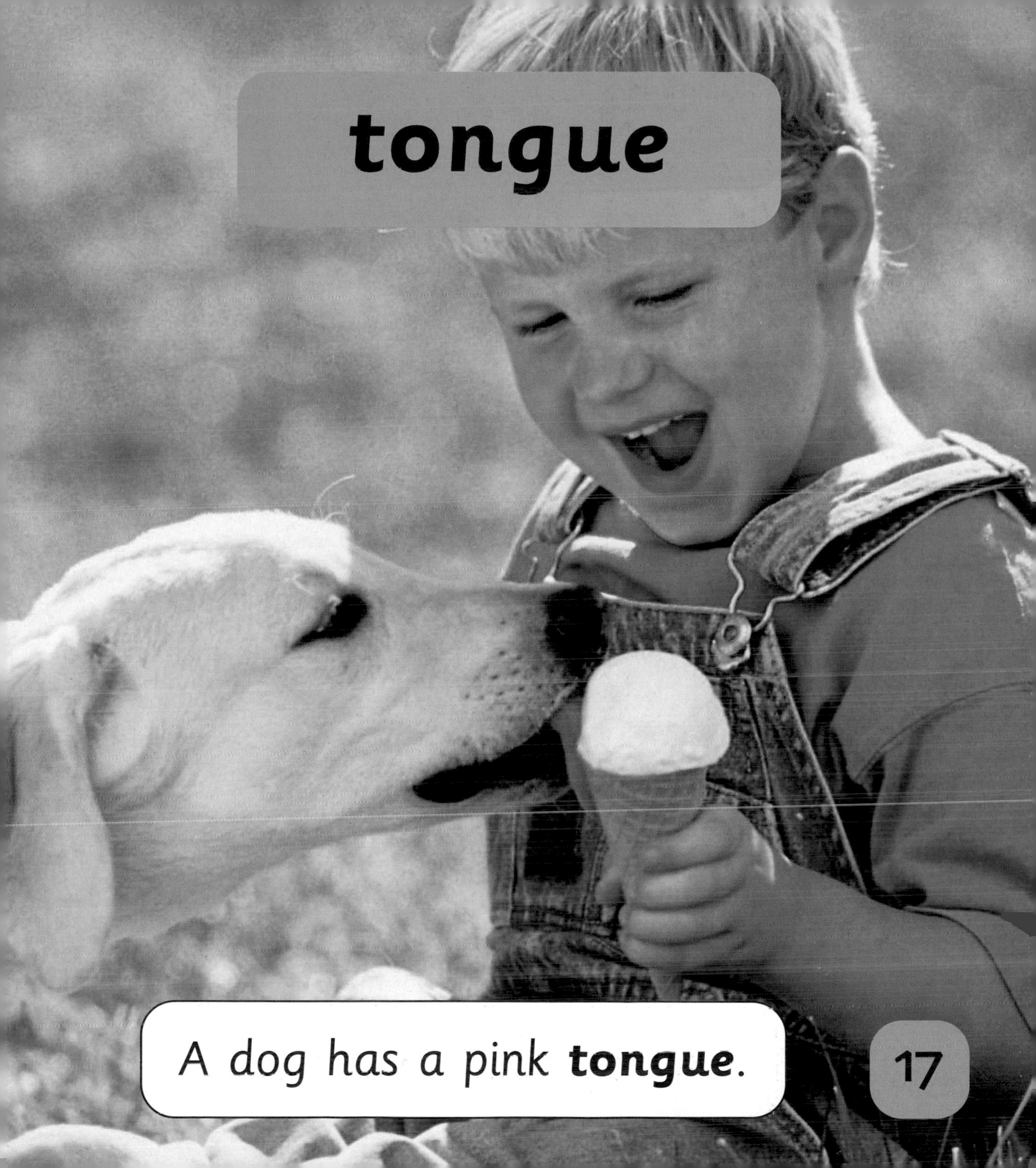

tongue

A dog has a pink **tongue**.

sheep dog

Some dogs work.

A **sheep dog** herds sheep.

What am I?

tongue

tail

nose

paw

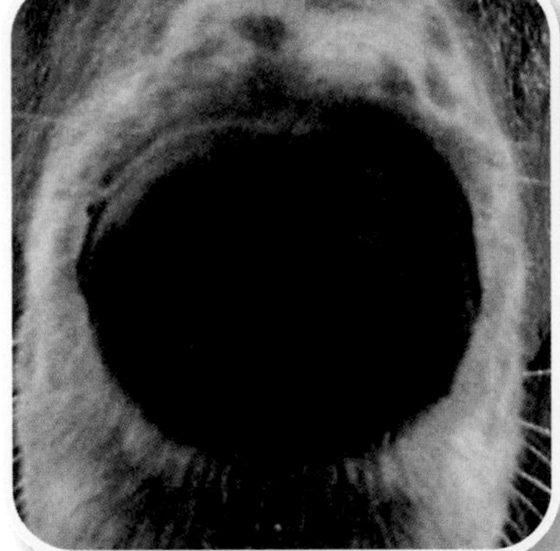

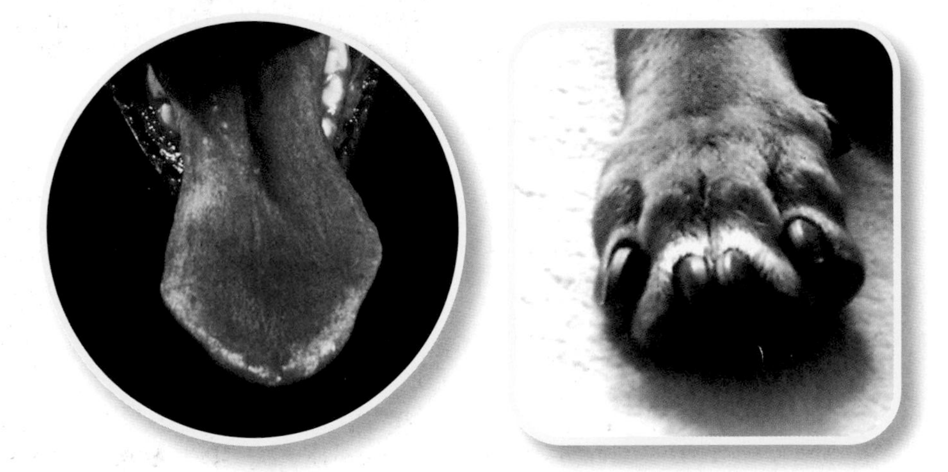

Match the words and pictures.

How many?

Can you count the dogs?

What noise?

Woof!

Growl!

Pant!

Slurp!

Can you sound like a dog?

Index

Can you find these dog pictures in the book?

For Parents and Teachers

Questions you could ask:

p. 2 How are these dogs different? Ask reader to compare size, shape, colour, fur of three dogs. Big dogs may be over 1m high and 1.5m long.

p. 4 What games do dogs like to play? This dog is catching a ball. Dogs also like fetching a stick, playing in water, tug-of-war.

p. 6 Does a puppy look like its parents? Yes, it looks the same, but it's smaller! Compare with baby animals that change, e.g. caterpillar, tadpole.

p. 8 What colour are dogs? Brown, black, white etc. Look at page 21 for variety. Describe unusual colours/patterns, e.g. Red Setter, Dalmatian.

p. 11 Could you run as fast as a dog? No! Some dogs are very fast, e.g. greyhounds.

p. 13 Why do you think dogs like to dig? They may be looking for food – they like to bury bones.

p. 15 What is this dog doing? Walking through the snow. This kind of dog (St. Bernard) is trained to look for people who have got lost in the mountains.

p. 16-17 What are these dogs doing? Sniffing/licking ice cream – dogs have a great sense of smell, e.g. sniffer dogs.

p. 18 What other jobs can dogs do? Guide dogs for the blind, sniffer dogs, police dogs, rescue dogs, dogs that pull sleds (see page 1). Some dogs act in movies!

Activities you could do:

- Ask the reader to draw dogs in different colours and patterns, e.g. Dalmatian, brown, black dogs.
- Role play – encourage the reader to act out how to look after a dog/puppy, e.g. feeding, cleaning, taking it for a walk, giving it a place to sleep etc.
- Read aloud dog stories, e.g. Kipper, Spot, Lassie.
- When you are out and about, look out for different types of dog. Ask the child to describe/ compare each dog, e.g. its colour, size, and shape.
- Introduce dogs by singing songs such as: "How much is that doggy in the window?" or "One man and his dog went to mow a meadow".

Paperback Edition 2009

Designed and produced by
Aladdin Books Ltd
PO Box 53987
London SW15 2SF

First published in 2006
by Franklin Watts
338 Euston Road
London NW1 3BH

Franklin Watts Australia
Level 17/207 Kent Street
Sydney NSW 2000

Franklin Watts is a division of Hachette Children's Books, an Hachette Livre UK company.
www.hachettelivre.co.uk

ISBN 978 0 7496 8971 1

A catalogue record for this book is available from the British Library.

Dewey Classification: 636.7

Printed in Malaysia

Series consultant
Zoe Stillwell is an experienced Early Years teacher currently teaching at Pewley Down Infant School, Guildford.

Photocredits*:*
l-left, r-right, b-bottom, t-top, c-centre, m-middle
All photos from istockphoto.com except: 6, 17, 20bl, 22bl & br — Comstock. 14-15, 20tl, 23br — Corbis.